MW00928010

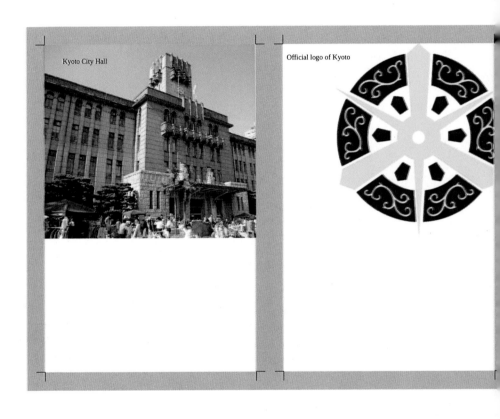

Kyoto City Hall

Official logo of Kyoto

Tori Japanese Shrine Torii Black And White

Kyoto Japan Statue Jizo Japanese Religion Culture

Beauty Geisha Asia Sensuality Japan Red

Architecture Japan Kyoto Path Shinto Temple Red

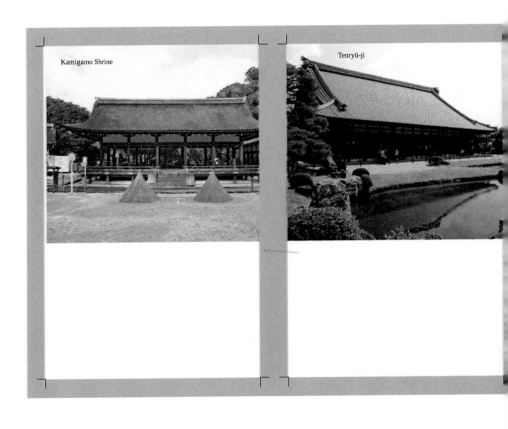

Kamigamo Shrine

Tenryū-ji

Lanterns Asian Japanese Red Glowing Ancient Asia

Japanese Asia Foliage Ancient Nature Trees Zen

inkaku Ji Snow Backlight

Japan Kyoto Arashiyama Asia Travel Temple

Japan Kyoto Kiyomizu-Dera Japanese Asia Landmark

Kinkaku-Ji Temple Kyoto Japan

Kinkakuji Kyoto Golden Pavilion Japan Zen Temple

Fushimi Inari-Taisha Shrine Kyoto Japan Temple

Kinkaku-Ji Temple Kyoto Japan

Beauty Asia Seductive Pretty Bridal Celebrate

Japan Shrine Kyoto Ewa Tourism History Scenic

Torii Kyoto Japan Shrine Kyoto Prefecture

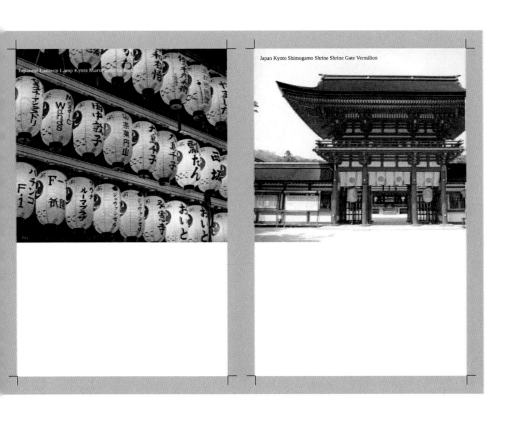

Japanese Lantern Lamp Kyoto Maruyama-Koen

Japan Kyoto Shimogamo Shrine Shrine Gate Vermilion

Kyoto The Scenery Temple Asia Roof Trees

Stone Path Stairs Forest Japan Kyoto Moss Nature

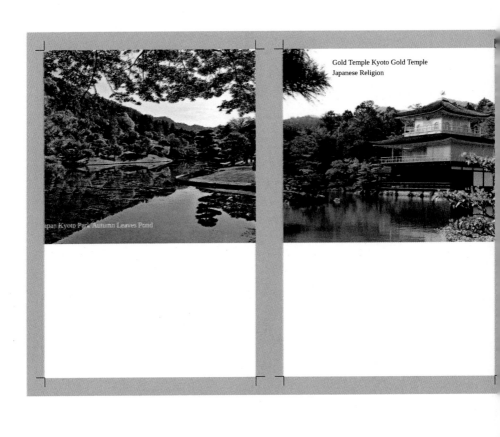

Gold Temple Kyoto Gold Temple
Japanese Religion

Japan Kyoto Park Autumn Leaves Pond

Temple Japan Kyoto Japanese Buddhist architecture

Kyoto Japan Kiyomizu Temple Asia Japanese Landmark

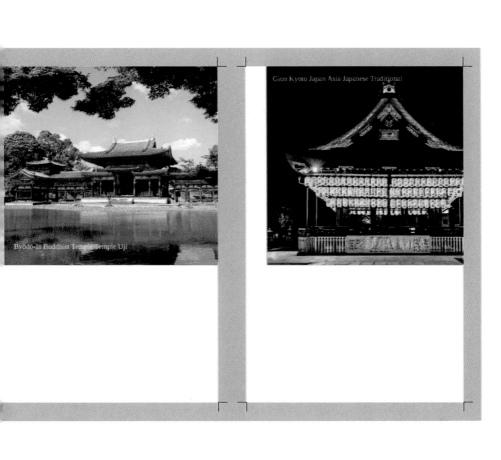

Byōdō-in Buddhist Temple Temple Uji

Gion Kyoto Japan Asia Japanese Traditional

Kyoto Japan Japanese Landmark Architecture Culture

Heian Shrine Torii Gate Kyoto Japan Sky C

Temple Garden Goal Kyoto Japan Zen Architecture

Kyoto Japan Temple Japanese Style

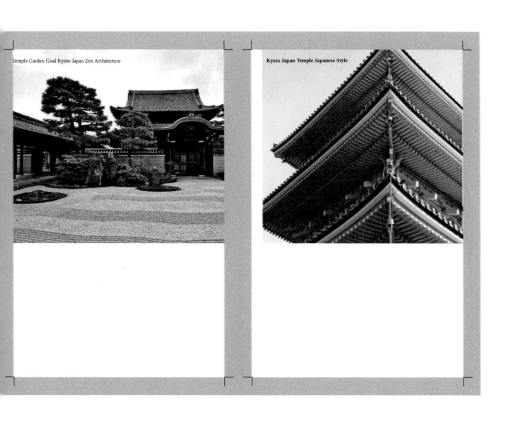

Japan Japanese Asia Oriental East Architecture

Japan Arashiyama School Children Uniforms People

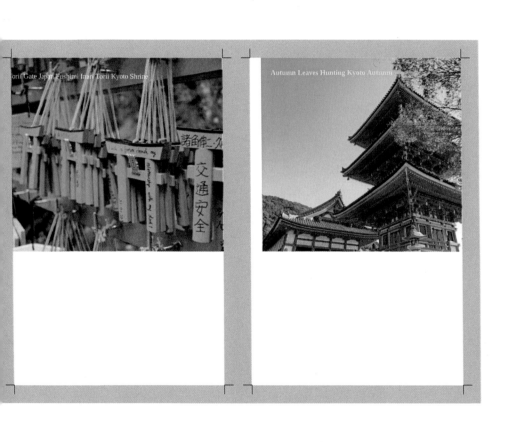

Kyoto Temple Japan Traditional Tourism Famous

Japan Kyoto Autumn Temple Garden Architecture

Pagoda Japan Kyoto Architecture Buddhist Temple

Japan Kyoto Sakura Spring

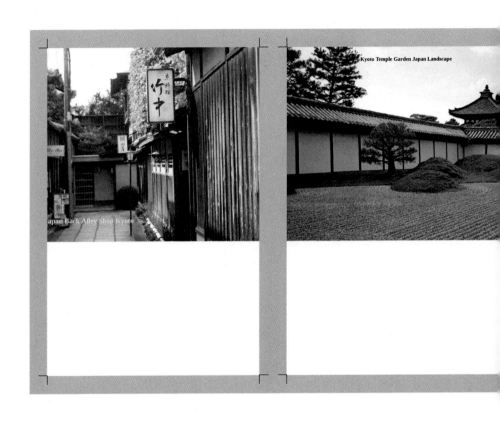

Kyoto Temple Garden Japan Landscape

Japan Back Alley Shop Kyoto

Kyoto Shrine Japan Kyoto Prefecture Buddhist

Japan Kyoto Girl Ice School Uniform Human Smile

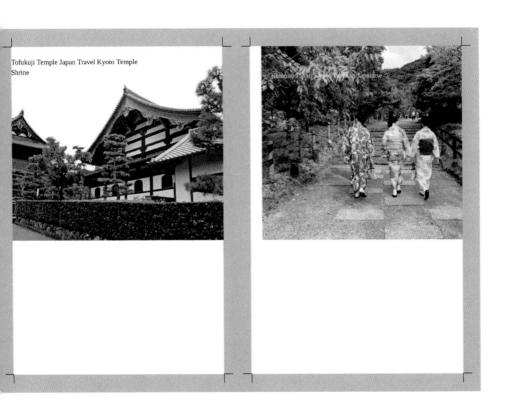

Tofukuji Temple Japan Travel Kyoto Temple Shrine

Kimono Japan Kyoto Woman Japanese

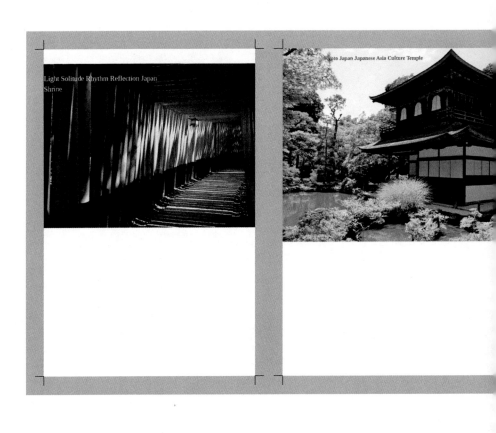

Light Solitude Rhythm Reflection Japan Shrine

Kyoto Japan Japanese Asia Culture Temple

Eikan Do Kyoto Temple

Japan Kyoto Religion Goldentemple Buddhism Asia

Road Path Tunnel Pattern Gravel Torii

World Heritage Of Seoul Tadashi Of The Ancestral Mausoleum

Japanese Garden Tree Houston Texas Flower Garden

Kyoto Sightseeing Temple

Japan Woman Music Tradition Asia Traditional

Kinkaku-Ji The Golden Pavilion Rokuon-Ji Zen Kyoto

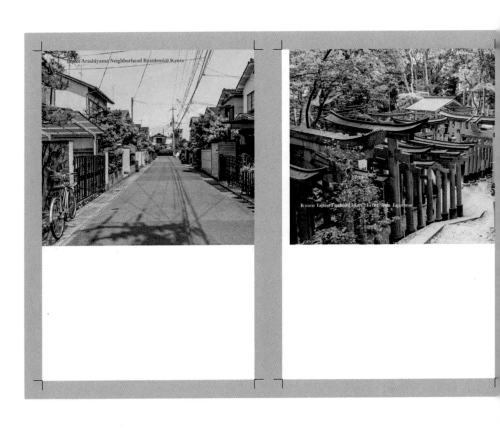

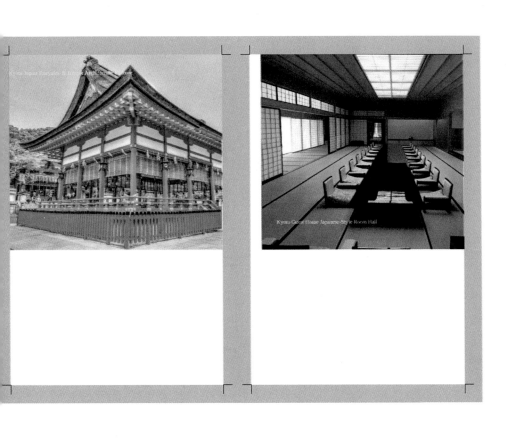

Kiyomizudera Temple Kyoto Japan Landmark Travel

Kyoto Japan Kiyomizu Temple Asia Japanese Landmark

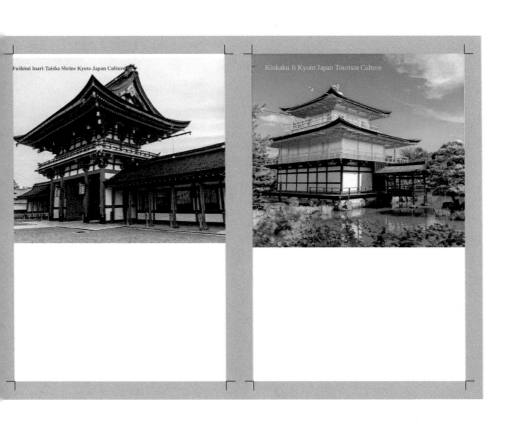

Fushimi Inari-Taisha Shrine Kyoto Japan Culture

Kinkaku Ji Kyoto Japan Tourism Culture

Japan Kyoto Temple Garden Autumn Leaves

Kyoto Japan Japanese Style Alley Japan House

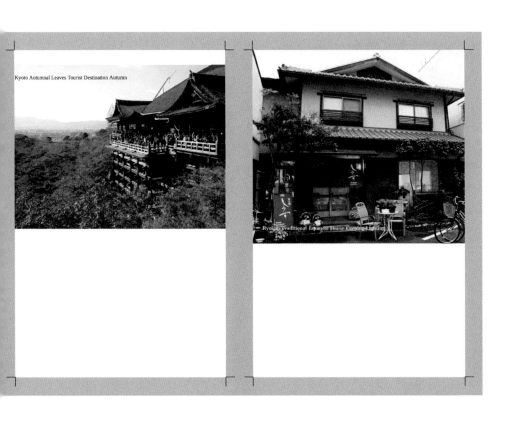

Japan Gion Kyoto Yasaka-Jinja Shrine Architecture

Kyoto Matcha Green Tea Break

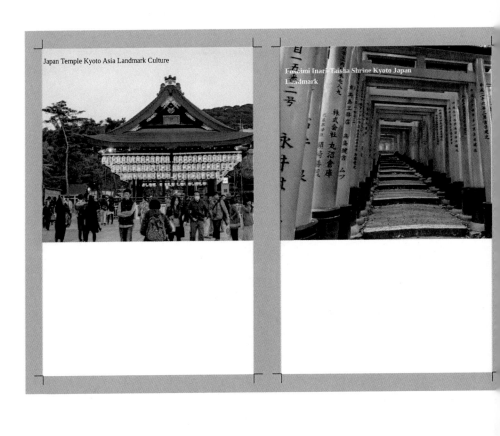

ushimi Inari-Taisha Shrine Kyoto Kyoto

Japan Kyoto Garden Heian Sanctuary Temple

Kyoto It Byodoin Temple Temples And Shrines Phoenix

Japan City Nijo Castle Kyoto Ping Cheng

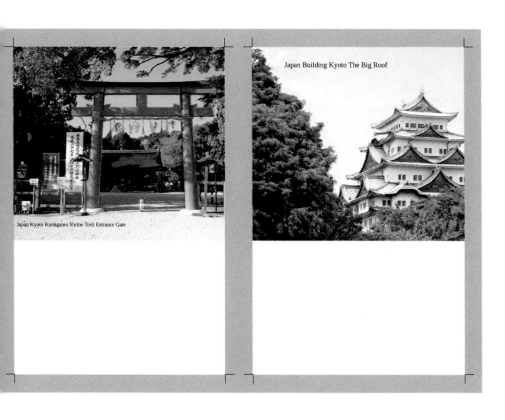

Japan Building Kyoto The Big Roof

Japan Kyoto Kamigamo Shrine Torii Entrance Gate

Temple Ancient Kyoto Japan Historic

Japan Kyoto The Big Roof Building

Fushimiinari Kyoto Geisha Religion Japan
Buddhist

Any Person Not Stage Wood Building Kyoto
Torii

Japan Arashiyama Landscape Kyoto Trees Nature

Arashiyama Japan Monkey Park Monkey Kyoto Wild

Kyoto Arashiyama Katsuragawa Togetsukyo
Winter

Kyoto Pagoda Japan Japanese Temple Shrine

Kyoto Japan Temple Bonsai Zen

Heian Shrine Kyoto Temple

Heian Jingu Shrine Shrine Kyoto

Kyoto Travel Byodoin Tourist Destination Tourism

Kyoto Japan Far East

River Kyoto Japan Far East

Kyoto Japan Cityscape City Mountain
Landscape

Japan Kyoto Japanese Landmark Travel
Asia

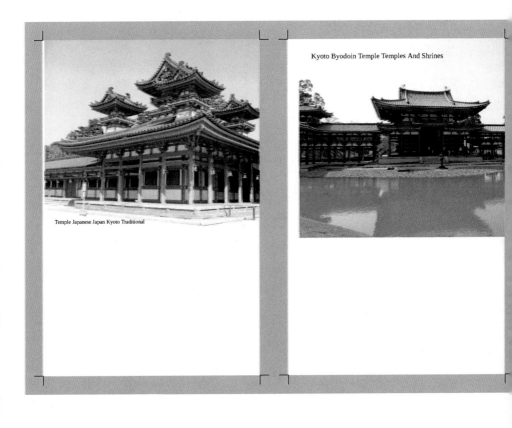

Kyoto Byodoin Temple Temples And Shrines

Temple Japanese Japan Kyoto Traditional

Kyoto Japan Japanese Landmark Travel Asia Template

Japan Kyoto Fushimi Inari Shrine Sky Japan Culture

Japan Kyoto Arashiyama Unesco Ten Categories

Pull Carts Rickshaw Kiyomizu Kyoto

Proof

Made in the USA
Las Vegas, NV
17 January 2022